Machines at Work

Diggers

by Cari Meister

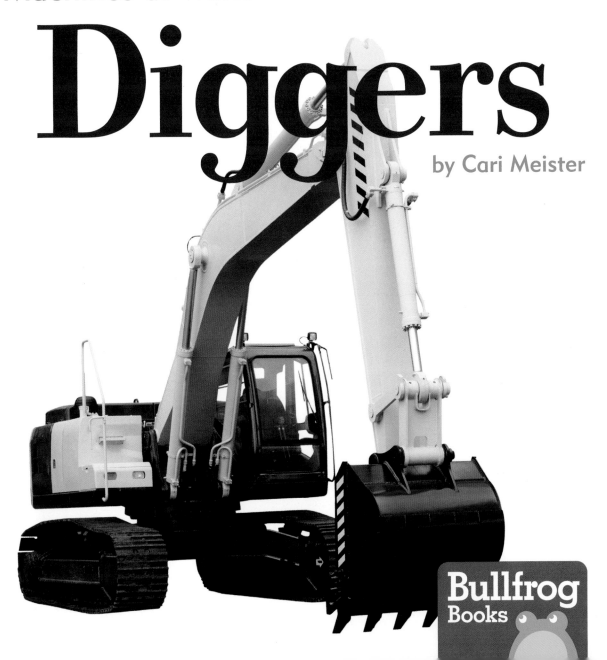

Bullfrog Books

Ideas for Parents and Teachers

Bullfrog Books let children practice reading informational text at the earliest reading levels. Repetition, familiar words, and photo labels support early readers.

Before Reading

- Discuss the cover photo. What does it tell them?
- Look at the picture glossary together. Read and discuss the words.

Read the Book

- "Walk" through the book and look at the photos. Let the child ask questions. Point out the photo labels.
- Read the book to the child, or have him or her read independently.

After Reading

- Prompt the child to think more. Ask: Have you ever seen a digger? Do you know what the digger was being used for?

Bullfrog Books are published by Jump!
5357 Penn Avenue South
Minneapolis, MN 55419
www.jumplibrary.com

Library of Congress Cataloging-in-Publication Data

Names: Meister, Cari.
Title: Diggers / by Cari Meister.
Description: Minneapolis, Minnesota: Jump!, Inc [2017]
Series: Machines at work | Audience: Age 5–8.
Audience: K to Grade 3.
Includes index.
Identifiers: LCCN 2016002945 (print)
LCCN 2016012247 (ebook)
ISBN 9781620313671 (hardcover: alk. paper)
ISBN 9781620314852 (paperback)
ISBN 9781624964145 (ebook)
Subjects: LCSH: Excavating machinery—Juvenile literature.
Classification: LCC TA732 .M45 2017 (print)
LCC TA732 (ebook) | DDC 621.8/65—dc23
LC record available at http://lccn.loc.gov/2016002945

Editor: Jenny Fretland VanVoorst
Series Designer: Ellen Huber
Book Designer: Leah Sanders
Photo Researcher: Leah Sanders

Photo Credits: All photos by Shutterstock except: Getty, 4, 5, 6–7, 18–19; Thinkstock, 16, 23tl.

Printed in the United States of America at Corporate Graphics in North Mankato, Minnesota.

Table of Contents

Diggers at Work   4

Parts of a Digger   22

Picture Glossary   23

Index   24

To Learn More   24

Diggers at Work

Ed puts on a hard hat.
He puts on ear muffs.

Ed drives an excavator.

He is going to work.

5

He gets in the cab.

He pushes a button.

Vroom!

The engine roars.

Ed pulls a lever.

The boom moves.

lever

It goes up.
It goes down.

9

bucket

Ed pulls another lever.
It moves the bucket.

Ed digs and digs.

He makes a giant hole.

It is the start
of a tall building.

Amy drives a backhoe.
It is smaller than
Ed's digger.

But it can do big jobs!

Amy digs and digs.
She scoops.

She dumps.

She makes a big hole.

Soon it will be a pool.

Diggers do good work!

Parts of a Digger

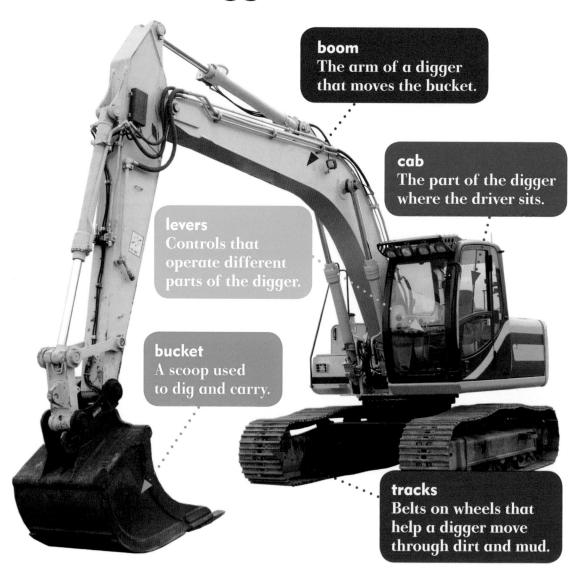

boom
The arm of a digger that moves the bucket.

cab
The part of the digger where the driver sits.

levers
Controls that operate different parts of the digger.

bucket
A scoop used to dig and carry.

tracks
Belts on wheels that help a digger move through dirt and mud.

Picture Glossary

backhoe
A digger that has a bucket and a loader.

engine
A machine that changes fuel into movement.

ear muffs
Covers that go over a driver's ears to protect them from loud noises.

excavator
A very big digger.

Index

backhoe 15

boom 8

bucket 11

cab 7

digging 12, 16

ear muffs 4

engine 7

excavator 5

hard hat 4

hole 12, 19

lever 8, 11

scooping 16

To Learn More

Learning more is as easy as 1, 2, 3.

1) Go to www.factsurfer.com

2) Enter "diggers" into the search box.

3) Click the "Surf" button to see a list of websites.

With factsurfer.com, finding more information is just a click away.